A Walk Thru the Book of

RUTH

Loyalty and Love

Walk Thru the Bible

BakerBooks

a division of Baker Publishing Group
Grand Rapids, Michigan

© 2009 by Walk Thru the Bible

Published by Baker Books
a division of Baker Publishing Group
P.O. Box 6287, Grand Rapids, MI 49516-6287
www.bakerbooks.com

Printed in the United States of America

Library of Congress Cataloging-in-Publication Data
A walk thru the book of Ruth : loyalty and love / Walk Thru the Bible.
        p.   cm.
    Includes bibliographical references.
    ISBN 978-0-8010-7169-0 (pbk.)
    1. Bible. O.T. Ruth—Study and teaching. 2. Bible. O.T. Ruth—Criticism, in-
terpretation, etc. I. Walk Thru the Bible (Educational ministry).
    BS1315.55.W36 2009
    222′.350071—dc22   2008050832

Cover image: ozgurdonmaz / iStock

Contents

Introduction

Chris Gardner was as low as he could get. Homeless, a single dad, and jobless, he had nowhere to go but up. But few people were willing to help him move in that direction. Through determination, persistence, and hard work, he eventually got an unpaid internship at a stock brokerage firm, earned a solid income, and got promoted again and again. By the end of the story, he was very successful and very wealthy. He had gone from rags to riches through strength of character and relentlessly pursuing unlikely opportunities.

That's the Chris Gardner from the film *The Pursuit of Happyness* (based on the real-life experience of a successful broker by the same name). It's one of those feel-good stories of a destitute and hopeless person who ends up bountifully blessed and fulfilled. While many of these sorts of stories teach a pull-yourself-up-by-the-bootstraps message, the book of Ruth tells a different story. Ruth positions herself to receive God's blessing through her commitment and hard work, but God is the one whose plans prevails in the end. By the end, both she and her mother-in-law, Naomi, have gone from hopeless poverty to abundant and lasting life.

Background

Ruth was probably written during the time of David. The genealogy at the end of the book includes him but goes no further. The events themselves, however, took place about a century before David during the time of the Judges, while Israel was still without a king. That period lasted around three hundred years, so Ruth and Boaz would have to have been married toward the end of that era in order to be David's great-grandparents.

While Naomi, Ruth, and Boaz were alive, life in the Promised Land didn't seem as promising as Israel had hoped. There were reasons for this; God had given quite specific instructions for being his chosen people—along with promises of abundant blessings for obedience and dire consequences for disobedience—yet the people of Israel had not followed him wholeheartedly. In fact, after the first generation in the Promised Land died off, Israelites forgot what God had done for them and let their hearts get caught up in the idolatry indigenous to Canaan. They experienced a cyclical pattern of disobedience, then judgment, then desperate prayers for deliverance, then deliverance, then apathy again. It was seen as a lawless time—Israel's version of the old American West, where law-abiding citizens were often overshadowed by those who made their own laws. The kingship of God was easily forgotten for long periods of time.

The book of Ruth is an unusual glimpse of real life during these times. Unlike most of biblical history, which is told from priestly, political, or military perspectives, Ruth takes place in a simple rural context and is told from a woman's point of view. This isn't the story a great historian would tell; it's an inside look at the everyday life of common people. In fact, it preaches a message to those who think history is determined by the rich and powerful: the story of God's kingdom is orchestrated by God himself, and absolutely anyone, no matter how unlikely, can take center stage in his plans. Israel's greatest kings, it tells us, descended not from the judges God used to win military victories, but from a couple of marginalized widows who were faithful in everyday life. Just as God would demonstrate centuries later in a manger in this very same town, he frequently uses humble means to accomplish great plans.

Major Themes

Ruth is a book of virtues. There are no parted seas or crumbling enemy walls, only the subtler miracle of ordinary people living out their faith and seeing God respond to it. The book commends to its readers the virtues of loyalty, hospitality, commitment, hard work, and obedience to the finer technicalities of God's law. For people who live according to God's own character, purposes, and ways, blessings eventually flow in and through their lives.

On the human side, one of the dominant themes of Ruth is restoration. We meet characters who have lost everything important to them and cling to God anyway. In their lives we see clear movements from emptiness to fullness; from aimlessness to direction; from temporal frustration to eternal significance; from hopelessness to purpose; from impossible to already done; and from loneliness to love. In these intertwined stories of provision, protection, and redemption, we find encouragement to believe that God will meet us in our moments of need and answer us beyond our wildest hopes.

The major theological theme of Ruth is God's sovereignty over circumstances as he orchestrates even minor details—such as which field someone happens to find work in, for example. The text rarely attributes the specifics of the plot to him—not explicitly, anyway—but the implication is that he is working behind the scenes the whole time. In many ways, it's a visual portrait of Romans 8:28: of all things working together for the good of those who love him and have been called according to his purpose.

How to Use This Guide

The questions in this guide are geared to elicit every participant's input, regardless of his or her level of preparation. Obviously, the more group members prepare by reading the biblical text and the background information in the study guide, the more they will get out of it. But even in busy weeks that afford no preparation time, everyone will be able to participate in a meaningful way.

The discussion questions also allow your group quite a bit of latitude. Some groups prefer to briefly discuss the questions in order to cover as many as possible, while others focus only on one or two of them in order to have more in-depth conversations. Since this study is designed for flexibility, feel free to adapt it according to the personality and needs of your group.

Each session ends with a hypothetical situation that relates to the passage of the week. Discussion questions are provided, but group members may also want to consider role-playing the scenario or setting up a two-team debate over one or two of the questions. These exercises often cultivate insights that wouldn't come out of a typical discussion.

Regardless of how you use this material, the biblical text will always be the ultimate authority. Your discussions may take you to many places and cover many issues, but they will have the greatest impact when they begin and end with God's Word itself. And never forget that the Spirit who inspired the Word is in on the discussion too. May he guide it—and you—wherever he wishes.

A Lawless Land

It didn't work out, and now she was depressed. Jan thought she had been trusting in God's promise—she even thought she'd heard him confirm his will again and again. But the promise never came, and her difficult circumstances had grown more difficult. Had she misunderstood his Word or misheard his voice? Had she missed God's blessing because of something she did wrong—or something she was supposed to do but didn't? Were her sins separating her prayers from the God who hears them? Perhaps she just didn't have enough faith. Or worse: perhaps God wasn't even there. No, that couldn't be it. She had experienced his work in her life so many times before. Her situation was simply an enigma. A draining, depressing enigma. She expected God to show up, and she wondered why he still hadn't—and why he remained so seemingly distant and detached in her crisis.

Most Christians have those thoughts on occasion, usually in a crisis in which we think God could have and should have intervened. Like it or not, we all seem to experience a relational gap between God and ourselves during certain seasons of life. When we do, we start to question the ground rules. "Did I not understand him? Did I break his rules? Am I not praying the right way? Am I his problem child?"

The truth we eventually come to grips with is that God doesn't spare his people from the hardships of this world, as Job and numerous other biblical characters testify. He does, however, give us plenty of guidance about how to avoid some of those hardships, how to navigate through the ones we can't avoid, and how to demonstrate faithfulness and godliness in spite of them. He also gives us plenty of promises about how he will keep us

THREE STORIES IN ONE

In many ways, the book of Ruth is really the story of Naomi, a Jew who lost her share of the Promised Land and had it restored in abundance. It's also the story of Boaz, a Jew who apparently had no heirs. Naomi, Ruth, and Boaz each had different needs, and God dealt with each of them as individuals. We can follow the distinct courses of his mercy: he brought Naomi from bitterness over loss to a completely restored inheritance; he gave the loyal outsider Ruth a permanent home among God's people; and he established a lasting legacy for the kind but lonely Boaz.

	Naomi	Ruth	Boaz
Chapter 1	Bitterness	Commitment	
Chapter 2	Provision	Courtship	Hospitality
Chapter 3	Security	Betrothal	Responsibility
Chapter 4	Inheritance	Marriage	Legacy

from ultimate harm and will bring us safely into his presence to dwell forever with him, where there are "eternal pleasures" (Ps. 16:11). He has not been silent. And by the time of Ruth, his voice had already been heard on these issues. The Torah had set the context for all that would happen in the family of Naomi and Ruth.

The Inheritance: Leviticus 25:23–28; Numbers 27:8–11

The law was aimed at keeping the land as close to its original owner as possible. If a man lost his piece of Israel's promised inheritance, his family members were to try to redeem it. If the family members couldn't, the tribe must. And if the original owner remained alive and regained his wealth, the subsequent owners were obligated to sell the land back to him. Whatever the cost, through however many generations, the promise must not be lost.

These commands are central to understanding the book of Ruth. Naomi's family hadn't just lost their land. They had lost their share in God's inheritance, and the rest of the story is a tender portrayal of God's desire to restore it.

Discuss

- Has God entrusted you with a heritage of any sort? How could you pass it on to future generations?

_____

_____

_____

_____

_____

_____

NAMES PAINT A PICTURE

As is often the case in Scripture, the names of characters in Ruth add color to the story. The book begins with a man named Elimelech ("God is king") who, ironically, took his wife Naomi ("beautiful and pleasant") out of the Promised Land and into Moab ("of his father," i.e., Lot), the land of corruption. Their two sons, Mahlon ("sickness") and Chilion ("failed"), married women of that land who were named Orpah ("stubborn") and Ruth ("friendship"). Eventually, after all the men died, Naomi ("beautiful and pleasant") called herself Mara ("bitter") upon returning to her hometown, Bethlehem (the "house of bread"), which was in the beginning stages of a grain harvest. But in that place, Ruth ("friendship") married a man named Boaz ("strong and quick"), and they bore children and grandchildren and a noteworthy great-grandchild named David ("beloved friend")—a king of Israel and a man after God's own heart.

The Fruitfulness: Deuteronomy 11:13–17

God promised abundance to those who keep his commands wholeheartedly. Rain would come in its proper seasons, and the land would produce a bountiful harvest. On the other hand, those who deviate from the paths he set them on were warned of famine and futility. Though this may not have been a one-to-one correlation—there have always been righteous people who suffer and wicked people who prosper for a time—the dynamic was certainly true for Israel as a whole. When people align themselves with God's will, his blessings flow more freely. When they don't, correction comes before more pleasant blessings.

This too is integral to understanding the book of Ruth. It's easy for us to miss the implications of Ruth 1:1, but for people who were living in the Promised Land, it would have been a major statement. In the mind of the Hebrew reader, there would be a reason for the famine, which would set the tone for the redemption to follow.

Discuss

- Do you think this principle of obedience leading to blessing applies to Christians today? Churches? Nations? Why or why not?

  _____

  _____

  _____

  _____

The Family Line: Deuteronomy 25:5–10

In a land of promise, where being part of God's kingdom means having part of God's estate, passing down an inheritance is vital. Not to build and maintain a heritage for future generations would be tantamount to removing yourself from the royal family. So when a man died without heirs . . . well, for many that was a tragedy worse than the death itself. The Promised Land had been won for every Israelite. It should never be lost for any of them.

The redemption and restoration found in Ruth make little sense without a firm understanding of this law. God's desire was for his blessings to extend to a thousand generations—in other words, forever. When those blessings were threatened in the life of a family, he expected other members of the community to do whatever they could to preserve that family's share of the promise. Primarily, the nearest male relative of a man who died was obligated to become the "kinsman-redeemer," the *go'el,* if the deceased was childless and the widow could still bear children. The purpose was to establish a heritage in the name of the departed. Otherwise, a lineage could be "blotted out" from the people of God. But beyond providing children, the extended family and the community at large were to protect the family's interests. The land and the lineage were sacred.

Discuss

- Cain had once declared that he was not his brother's keeper (Gen. 4:9). But when God established Israel, he assured them that they *were* each other's keepers. What aspects of this sort of communal caretaking do you see in today's church? What aspects are missing?

_____

_____

_____

_____

The Problem: Judges 2:10–19; 21:25

The period of the Judges is depicted as a cycle of lawlessness that led to oppression that led to repentance that led to deliverance that resulted in lawlessness again. For most of those three centuries, the people to whom God had given very specific instructions "did what was right in [their] own eyes." It was a time of missed blessings.

That's when the story of Ruth takes place. We don't know the exact timing during that period, but chances are that lovers of God's law were few and far between. Consequently, life was harder than it should have been. But the message of the book is that God's covenant blessings still apply to faithful people even when those around them don't "get it." He always honors heartfelt obedience, regardless of the lawless surroundings in which he finds it.

Discuss

- How difficult do you find it to be faithful to God in our culture? Can you think of examples in our own culture where "everyone does what is right in his or her own eyes"?

_____

_____

_____

_____

A CASE STUDY

Imagine: This is the most excruciating season of your life. Your spouse's yearlong battle with cancer ended last month, and you're devastated. During the turmoil of the past year, you lost your job and all your savings. Now you're in debt up to your ears, bill collectors call you relentlessly, and your home is being turned over to public auction. You've tried to be faithful to God during the whole mess, but it's hard; you wonder where he is—or even *if* he is. If he's the God you've always believed in, he could have stepped in and delivered your spouse—and you—at any moment he wanted. Still, in the midst of your utter ruin, he waits.

- Would you be more tempted to blame God for your problems or to feel guilty for some unknown sin he must be chastising you for? Why?
- What questions would you ask him? How much would your commitment to him waver when he seems less than committed to you?
- What truths would help you focus on the big, eternal picture rather than on your present circumstances?

A Tragic Family

RUTH 1

Naomi was the worst kind of widow. Every woman in the ancient Middle East was under the guardianship of a man as his daughter, his wife, or his mother. But not Naomi. She is one of the few most unfortunate widows to be left without a single male guardian in her family. Her father is never mentioned—her age indicates that he had probably died long ago. Her husband dies in a foreign land, and her only two sons follow him to the grave in their prime of life. Homeless and destitute, she's the ancient version of a bag lady. And, because of her age, she has no hope of acquiring a guardian in the form of a husband and then a male heir—assuming, of course, that neither of her foreign daughters-in-law decides to remain with her.

19

THE MOABITE STIGMA

Centuries before Ruth, Lot and his two daughters were the only survivors of God's judgment on Sodom. The girls, whose fiancées had ignored warnings to flee, were alone with their father in the hills. With no apparent prospects of bearing children to carry on the family name, they took turns getting their father drunk and sleeping with him. They each bore a son, one of whom was named Moab.

The incestuous origin of the Moabite people was firmly fixed in the Israelite consciousness. For a Jew, Moab represented immorality and corruption. That image was reinforced in the wilderness as Moabite leader Balak hired Balaam to curse the Jews as they neared the Promised Land. Moabite women seduced Jewish men and influenced them to worship their idols, and Moab's obese King Eglon oppressed them for eighteen years. Israelites considered Moab to be a very unsavory place.

All Moabites inherited that stigma, which would have made Ruth a startling character to the story's original hearers. Elimelech, a Jew, had abandoned the Promised Land for Moab, and years later only two people returned: his faithful widow and a remarkable young non-Jew who had been born and raised in the land of corruption.

What difference would that unlikely turn of events make? An adoptive daughter would be able to get a husband and bear a son, and that would restore her firmly back in a patriarchal family, with inheritance and legacy intact. But what are the odds of that? Slim . . . virtually nonexistent . . . hopeless. Especially when the hopes are riding on non-Jewish daughters of Moab.

Widows don't suffer the same plight in most modern cultures today, but the human condition still affords plenty of opportunity for hopelessness. Relationships, health, finances, dreams for a better future—all can be demolished in one unfortunate blow, leaving us breathless, broken, and bereft of hope.

The testimony of the book of Ruth, and of the Bible as a whole, is that God is a master of impossible situations. In fact, he seems to delight in them. No matter how hopeless any season of our life gets, redemption and restoration are held before us for our faith to embrace. God gives promises for the destitute. He is with the brokenhearted. He protects and delivers the widows—even those in impossible situations.

Promised Land Lost: Ruth 1:1–7

"There was a famine in the land, and a man from Bethlehem in Judah, together with his wife and two sons, went to live for a while in the country of Moab." That may seem like a simple scene-setting statement to us, but it was loaded with meaning to its first readers. The fact that there was a famine in the Promised Land meant that God was disciplining his people for disobedience and idolatry—a fulfillment of Deuteronomy 11:13–17. If fertile fields had turned to dry dust, Israel had departed from the ways of God.

Considering the time in which Naomi and Ruth lived, in which lawlessness ruled the day, that's not surprising. But the second half of the statement is just as alarming. Elimelech, a man from the tribe of Judah, took his family and left the Promised Land in search of greener pastures. God had set his people apart with miraculously provided land and entrusted them with the revelation of his character and his ways. And when the land ceased to yield its produce because of the people's idolatry, Elimelech decided not to stick it out—even though most people stayed and apparently survived anyway. In other

ORPAH'S GOD

Though all non-Jewish religions in and around the Promised Land were polytheistic, most identified with a primary national god. The god of Moab was Chemosh—a name meaning "destroyer" or "subduer." Long after Ruth, the king of Moab ended a losing battle against Israel by sacrificing his own son, the crown prince, to this god (2 Kings 3:26–27). A tablet from this period—the "Moabite Stone," or "Mesha Inscription"—explains the oppression by King Omri of Israel in religious terms from a Moabite perspective: Chemosh had become angry with his people and allowed them to become Israel's servants. And Israel called them "the people of Chemosh" too (Num. 21:9; Jer. 48:46). Moabites were identified with their dominant deity.

So when Naomi encourages Ruth and Orpah to go back to their people and then indicates that Orpah is returning to "her gods" (1:15), she's not only describing the religious background of her daughters-in-law; she's also making a significant theological statement. She seemingly recommends the worship of Chemosh the destroyer over the worship of Yahweh—who, as she will declare in the next few verses, has brought calamity and bitterness upon her. Ruth's response to Naomi and commitment to Naomi's God are, in effect, a counter-statement of faith in Yahweh over Chemosh.

words, he abandoned the promise because the covenant wasn't working for him.

Elimelech apparently died soon after, and his sons married Moabite women—a clear violation of God's law (Deut. 7:3–4). Then his sons died. Such calamity was, to the Hebrew reader, a plain indication that God was judging Elimelech and his sons for their bad decisions. All that remain of the family are three widows, only one of whom is a member of the people of God. And since God has restored rain to the homeland, she now decides to return.

Discuss

- What do you think of Elimelech's decision to abandon the Promised Land? What are some possible consequences of fleeing God's discipline in the way Elimelech did?

  _____

  _____

  _____

  _____

- Does God discipline today? If so, how? How do you think most Christians respond to his discipline, and how do you respond to it?

  _____

  _____

  _____

Promised Land Sought: Ruth 1:8–18

When a woman married, she literally transferred her sense of identity to her husband's family. She became a citizen of a different "clan" or tribe. Naomi tries to absolve her daughters-in-law of that responsibility—she was the only close family member left—because the law for providing them an heir cannot be fulfilled. Even if Naomi could have other sons through a second marriage—a most unlikely prospect at her age—Ruth and Orpah would have to wait about twenty years before bearing their children through levirate law. Elimelech's line seems to be completely cut off. The only hope Ruth and Orpah have for descendants, according to Naomi, is to return to their original family.

Orpah agrees with this logic, but Ruth doesn't. Or, if she does, she counts Naomi's welfare as more important than her own sense of fulfillment. She has developed some level of affinity for Israel's God and a remarkable level of devotion for her mother-in-law. In one of Scripture's most beautiful statements of loyalty, she pledges to leave everything behind and remain a member of the family she married into. In effect, she renounces her Moabite ancestry and identifies herself with God's chosen people.

Ruth and Orpah are pictures of the choices we all have to face: the familiar versus the unknown, security versus adventure, loving someone versus loving *and* being committed to someone. Or, to put it in terms of the gospel, simply admiring the family of God or choosing to stick with the family of God through thick and thin. And Ruth is held up as the nobler picture. Did she fear the wrath of Moab's gods by choosing Israel's God? Did she fear the discrimination and discomfort she might face in a foreign land? Was she tempted to seek a Moabite man so she could marry again? All we know is that she clung to Naomi—and her radical decision—and wouldn't let go.

Discuss

- Both Orpah and Ruth made a commitment to the family of their husbands, and then the circumstances changed. One of them regretfully backed away from the commitment, while the other deepened it. How do you view your commitments when the circumstances under which you made them change? Do you think Ruth's sense of loyalty and family honor is common among Christians today? If not, should it be?

  _____

  _____

  _____

  _____

- What did Ruth sacrifice in order to keep the commitment she made when she married? Do you think her Moabite friends would have seen her as noble or irrational? Why?

  _____

  _____

  _____

  _____

A Land Without Promise? Ruth 1:19–22

The people of Bethlehem rejoice to see their long-lost friend again, but in her grief, Naomi cries out against God. The Lord has afflicted her, abandoned her, stripped her of all that mattered to her. The rest of the book tells the story of how God answers this charge, but at the end of chapter 1, the suspense of the story is captured in these questions: Is this woman Naomi ("pleasant"), or is she Mara ("bitter")? What will God do with a woman whose eyes are rubbed raw from personal tragedy?

The deeper question, of course, is whether God will live up to his covenant. Will the faithful people in this story be vindicated? Will they be protected and preserved? Will the promised blessings come through in the end? Ruth, a foreigner, has looked at the impossible situation and cast her lot with the God of covenant anyway. Naomi, a Jew, has looked at the impossible situation and asked the hard questions about suffering. In the end, God will show his favor to both.

Discuss

- How do you respond to God when there's a long wait between suffering and redemption? What happens to your faith when a confusing detour takes you away from what you thought were God's plans?

_____

_____

_____

_____

• In what kinds of situations do you need God's promises most? In what kinds of situations are you least likely to trust them? Are there any similarities between the two?

_____

_____

_____

_____

A Case Study

Imagine: Your employer has always been good to you. The company gave you your first job even though you didn't feel qualified for it, they have always spent plenty of time and resources on your personal and professional development, they have been rather generous with bonuses and extra time off when you were going through a crisis, and they have proven their long-term commitment to you. Naturally, your loyalty to them is as strong as their loyalty to you.

But now they want to promote you, which would involve a transfer overseas to an unfamiliar country. They want you to commit to staying there through thick and thin—perhaps for the rest of your career. You'll leave behind your extended family, your church, your friends—even your favorite foods and clothes and pastimes. You'll have to learn a new language and adapt to a new culture. Though you feel obligated to say yes, venturing into the great unknown is more than a little unnerving.

- How strong would your sense of loyalty have to be to agree to this situation? What would it take for you personally to develop the kind of loyalty necessary for this sort of situation?
- Why do you think some people find it easy to leave their past behind and move on to something completely new? Why do you think some people find it nearly impossible?
- In what ways is making a commitment to Christ comparable to this situation?

A Place for a Stranger

RUTH 2

It certainly wasn't the first time Lalo had been harassed and ridiculed. That was a normal occurrence for those who work the citrus harvests. But this time was different. This time he was being intentionally distracted and overworked while his wife, Leti, suffered the aggressive advances of the foreman. If he reported the foreman's behavior to the landowner, it would have been the word of an illiterate immigrant against the word of a trusted farmhand. If he did nothing . . . well, he *had* to do something—for Leti's honor, for his children's respect, for his own peace of mind. So Lalo, Leti, and their two children packed their few possessions, left on foot in the middle of the night, and hoped the road would be more hospitable to a migrant family than their employer's men had been. There would be

GLEANINGS

Most farmers would consider it a matter of stewardship to harvest crops thoroughly and maximize their profits, but God commanded a degree of inefficiency. Why? Because the poor—foreigners, widows, orphans—would be wandering the land in search of food. If they were to be fed, some crops would have to be left behind.

God's compassion for people like Ruth—both an alien and a widow—is spelled out in Leviticus 19:9–10 and 23:22 and Deuteronomy 24:17–22. This was Israel's equivalent of a food pantry for the poor. Crops could not be gathered from the corners and edges of the fields, and any stalks that dropped in the sheaving process were to be left on the ground. Ruth had asked to gather from these leftovers (2:3, 7), but Boaz even encouraged her to glean from the middle of the fields and made sure she had plenty to find (2:15–16). His favor resulted in a rather large net take for a day's work—a full sack that would feed Naomi and her for weeks.

more harassment along the way, he was sure. And having to find another farm to work on in the middle of the season might raise questions about where he was coming from and why he had left. Still, he'd have to take the hard road because not to take it would be harder. As they say, beggars can't be choosers. Especially if the beggar is an alien in need of work.

Initially, Ruth would have had about the same amount of esteem in the barley fields as that of migrant workers like Lalo and Leti in today's agricultural economy. She had no status, no provider or protector to look out for her, and a distinctive accent betraying her Moabite background. If any man in the fields wanted someone to insult, to tease, or to have his own way with, she would be the prime candidate. She had no leverage, no means to defend herself, no legitimate threats of retaliation against an aggressor. And though God had told his people to care for aliens and widows, she lived in a day when "everyone did right in his own eyes." She was as vulnerable as a young woman can get.

If Boaz is a model of godly character—and he clearly is—kindness to those who are most vulnerable is a godly trait. It's one of the distinctives of God's people that we not only demonstrate hospitality when the need for it confronts us but that we go out of our way to find where hospitality is needed. Boaz inquired of Ruth's situation and went above and beyond the law's expectations in meeting her needs. He saw her lack of protection and provision and became her protector and provider by letting her gather in his fields and by issuing orders not to harass her. He did what Jesus does for us and what we should do for others.

HOSPITALITY

In the ancient Middle East, hospitality was more than a virtue; it was a system of survival for travelers in need of food, water, and shelter. There was an unstated reciprocal agreement to host strangers for short periods of time and to offer certain kinds of provisions. One's hospitality might grow more extravagant, depending on the status of either the host or the stranger. But addressing the basic needs of a traveler was assumed.

Even so, low-status strangers were sometimes overlooked anyway. After all, those having nothing with which to reciprocate often get left out of reciprocal agreements. But God insisted that there should be no low-status strangers among his people. "When an alien lives with you in your land, do not mistreat him. The alien living with you must be treated as one of your native-born. Love him as yourself, for you were aliens in Egypt. I am the LORD your God" (Lev. 19:33–34). Boaz went well beyond this command and, in the mind of Hebrew readers of Ruth, earned a reputation for being an extremely virtuous man.

30

Providence: Ruth 2:1–13

Though the text doesn't specifically say God arranged for Ruth to end up in Boaz's field, that's the obvious implication. He is behind the scenes, guiding Ruth into the right field during a busy harvest, when numerous other fields would have leftover gleanings too. As it turns out, Boaz is a relative in Elimelech's clan. He asks his workers who the new young woman belongs to—all women in that culture are under someone's guardianship—and he learns of Ruth's past, her strong loyalty to Naomi and the God of Israel, and her admirable work ethic. He blesses her and treats her as a member of the clan, not as an outsider.

Ruth demonstrates sincere humility, marveling that a man of fine standing would be so generous with a foreigner like her. And the blessing he pronounces over her is deeply symbolic, a picture not only of how God has responded to Ruth's faith, but also of how Boaz will be called upon to respond to her soon. On a larger scale, it's a dramatic picture of God's response to all who come to him in faith, whether Jew or Gentile, insider or outsider, prosperous or destitute. Even a Moabite can become one of God's people by reflecting God's character and trusting his purposes. And as the passage progresses, one begins to get the impression that the sovereign God is not only arranging provision for Ruth and Naomi. He's playing the role of a matchmaker.

Discuss

- Have you seen God work in the "random" choices you've made? If so, how?

_____

_____

_____

- Who in your community—racially, economically, linguistically, etc.—most closely correlates with the lowly status of a poor, outcast Moabite? Does your church show God's hospitality to them?

  _____

  _____

  _____

  _____

Potential: Ruth 2:14–23

As the day progresses, the emptiness of chapter 1 continues to disappear under the abundance of the harvest and Boaz's generosity. Ruth is allowed to eat to her heart's content at the same table with family, friends, and hired workers. Boaz ensures that she finds an abundance of grain, and she gathers a large amount to take home to Naomi. Her conversation with her mother-in-law is telling: while she recites the facts of the day and sees work potential, Naomi marvels that God's kindness still extends to her and sees marriage potential.

- What attitudes has Ruth demonstrated during her day in Boaz's fields? Which of her many needs has Boaz already met?

  _____

  _____

- At this point in the story, in what respects does Ruth represent people outside of God's kingdom? In what respects does Boaz represent Jesus?

  _____

  _____

A CASE STUDY

Imagine: She has cleaned the church for years—a thankless job, even among a thankful people—but you still don't know her name. Not many people do, apart from the staff who have to give her instructions and pay her wages. But one day you realize you haven't seen her face in a while. You ask the building manager where she is, and he says she was let go. It seems that a DVD player was taken from one of the classrooms, and all signs pointed to her as the culprit. No one knows where she is now.

- If you heard a report like this, would you make any assumptions of guilt or innocence? Why or why not?
- How concerned would you be for that person's welfare?
- How would you feel if you found out later that she, like Ruth, had a special destiny and was raised to a position of vital significance in God's kingdom?

Courage

RUTH 3

He had been waiting all his life for this moment. He nervously fumbled with the ring in his pocket and mentally rehearsed his lines once again. No matter how often he had discussed the possibility of marriage with her, he still wasn't sure she was ready. He wasn't even sure *he* was ready. He just knew how much he loved her and wanted to marry her. He believed this was how God had guided them. And he just hoped, with all his heart, that in this defining moment, she would have the nerve to say yes.

There comes a moment in every matter of faith when you have to put it all on the line. You stand at the edge of a Red Sea and pray for the water to open; you finish marching around a Jericho and come to the time to shout; you stand before a Goliath with a slingshot and five stones; or you get tired of running into a mountain and finally tell it to move. In many cases in Scripture, the moment of faith is a matter of life and death—at least of a dream or a heart, if not of a physical body. But in every case, the stakes are high. Either your faith will be vindicated or it will be destroyed. Your entire future, it seems, is on the line.

That must have been how it seemed to Ruth. Her welfare, as well as Naomi's, hinged on this request for marriage. But this was more than a matter of welfare; it was a matter of the heart. According to Boaz, Ruth could have made herself available to any young, single man in the fields, but she didn't. She chose him—the man who, it seems, had already chosen her as well.

If you ever wondered if God is concerned with matters of the heart, the story of Ruth is clear evidence that he is. He doesn't just provide for our material needs; he seeks our emotional fulfillment as well. He satisfies the desires of every living thing (Ps. 145:16). And he honors those who will approach a critical moment in complete faith that he guides, protects, provides, and fulfills.

The Big Risk: Ruth 3:1–6

Naomi plays the role of matchmaker—not entirely aware, of course, that God has already done so. The kinsman-redeemer will be sleeping on the threshing floor, as all male harvesters do to protect the harvest from thieves at night. Naomi devises a seductive plan involving perfume, pretty clothes, and a secret rendezvous. The men will have drunk enough to help them sleep well on the rough ground but not enough to sleep through the sound of rustling sheaves being stolen away. And for that small window of time, the kinsman-redeemer will be approachable in relative privacy—*if* his friends aren't restless.

35

ECHOES OF HER ANCESTRY

The sordid origins of Moab are described in Genesis 19:29–38—the story of Lot's incestuous episode with his daughters that spawned two nations. For those with an intimate knowledge of Scripture, the encounter between Boaz and this Moabite in the middle of the night has clear connotations of that event. But the moral tone in each incident makes for a dramatic contrast. In Genesis 19, the midnight encounter is deviant and illegitimate. In the story of Ruth, it's a romantic prelude to a noble and virtuous marriage. In effect, Boaz redeems more than the lives and inheritance of two widows; he also reverses the effects of a sin of the distant past.

If Boaz rejects her, the embarrassment won't be public for either of them. If she's spotted, however, the scandal could be enormous. Regardless, it's the best opportunity she'll have. In that unconventional time at that unconventional place, Ruth will invite a marriage proposal with a traditional gesture. The protocol is ordinary; the setting, anything but. It's a daring, provocative gambit.

Discuss

- Do you think it's possible to demonstrate faith without taking some kind of risk? Why or why not? How convinced of God's will do you generally have to be before stepping out in faith with a lot on the line?

_____

_____

_____

_____

_____

36

The Big Moment: Ruth 3:7–15

Boaz eats, drinks, and falls asleep. Ruth quietly approaches—there are other men nearby, and she can't afford to wake them. She lies down at Boaz's feet and uncovers them, setting the stage for the symbolic gesture of the groom: the spreading of his "wings" over his bride to cover her as her protector and provider. It's the same way the God of Israel covers his children (2:12), redeeming them from their captivity and restoring them into his family.

Boaz wakes in the middle of the night and notices a woman at his feet. It's a shocking discovery—women don't go out at night alone, and they certainly don't sleep on the threshing floor among men who have had a bit to drink. But Boaz isn't bothered by how the scene might affect his reputation. He marvels at Ruth's choice. She could have attracted younger men; she could have sought her own fulfillment rather than the redemption of Naomi's piece of God's promise; she could have passively waited

AND BOAZ TOO?

God's concern for two widows in need and a family's inheritance is clear in the themes of Ruth. But what about the kinsman-redeemer himself? There's no mention of a wife, children, or any sort of past or present family. From all appearances, Boaz has no one to inherit his portion of the Promised Land—until Ruth comes along and provides him with children. The book of Ruth is the story not only of the provision *of* a redeemer but also of God's provision *for* a redeemer.

Like Boaz, our Redeemer is in pursuit of a bride and a people to share in his inheritance. From all appearances, we approach him for our redemption, as though initiating the request is our responsibility. But, like Boaz, he has first invited us into his fields and fed us from his bounty. He has made his overtures and waits for our response.

for a proposal that might have never come. Instead, she pursued her heart's desire, her mother-in-law's welfare, and her adoptive culture's faith. She acted like an Israelite because of love.

Boaz is honored. Enamored. Enthusiastic for his new bride. But before she can be officially betrothed to him, the law must be observed. There's a protocol to be followed, and another kinsman-redeemer is in line. He has to be given an opportunity to redeem Naomi's latent field—and the foreign girl who comes with it. Meanwhile, he loads her down with grain to take back to Naomi. It's a sign of acceptance, a blessing of abundance, a symbol of fulfillment . . . and perhaps a ready-made explanation for a young woman walking home from the threshing floor at dawn.

Discuss

- As a single woman, Ruth risked danger walking to the threshing floor alone at night, and she risked scandal (and being ostracized) if someone saw her there. With that in mind, do you think her visit to Boaz was still appropriate and godly? Why or why not?

  _____

  _____

  _____

- In what ways might the marriage of Boaz and Ruth defy the expectations and sense of propriety of his friends and family? Are you open to the possibility of God working through unconventional means in your life?

  _____

  _____

  _____

The Big Victory: Ruth 3:16–18

Boaz is a gentleman, at least as Ruth portrays him to Naomi; she explains her bounty of barley as an expression of Boaz's desire that she not return to her mother-in-law empty-handed. Or perhaps he is already hinting at his willingness to endow the family with an appropriate bride-price. Either way, the chapter ends poetically in daylight with a garment full of grain. It's God's way of emphasizing a point: he fills empty places in our lives and shines light into dark seasons of life. The impossible situation of Naomi and Ruth is now on the verge of redemption.

Discuss

- In what ways is Ruth's request and Boaz's acceptance similar to our own salvation in Christ? In what ways is it different?

  _____

  _____

  _____

  _____

- What empty places or dark seasons in your life do you need God to redeem? How do you think he will respond to a Ruth-like request for his "covering"—that is, placing yourself at his feet and asking him to spread his provision and protection over you?

  _____

  _____

  _____

  _____

  _____

A CASE STUDY

Imagine: You have one shot to make an impression on the committee. You're amazed you even made it to this stage of the tryouts—it's an extremely selective program—but now you've gotten your hopes up. If you get in, the only career you ever dreamed of is laid out in front of you. If not . . . well, once-in-a-lifetime opportunities only come around once in a lifetime. You'll be devastated. It's now or never.

- How well do you handle intense, pressure-filled, high-stakes situations like this? Do you relish such opportunities or dread them?
- How easily do you place your burdens on God when you're facing a critical moment? To what degree are you able to rest in his sovereignty?
- If you were helping a friend prepare for such a moment, which of God's promises would you try to reassure him or her with? How have these promises comforted you in your crises?

What's Right in God's Eyes

RUTH 4

There was only one obstacle standing between Derek and his dream: the small matter of keeping his word. He was under contract at his current job and had pledged to fulfill the full length of his agreement. But that was before he got the job offer of a lifetime—a ministry position that fit his gifts perfectly and that he'd always felt called to do. All he had to do was retract his verbal pledge and buy out the terms of his contract. Though it would put his "secular" employer in a bind, the boss would certainly understand. That's the way of the business world. And if he waited to fulfill his agreement, the opportunity would probably pass. But the Spirit and his conscience kept reminding him that his "yes" was to be "yes" and his "no" was to be "no." It was a matter of integrity—and of the God who called him to ministry in the first place.

God frequently allows his people to come face-to-face with a shortcut to his plans. That's where real commitment to his character is demonstrated. Which is more important: the goals he has for us or the means to get there? It's a false choice, as both go hand in hand. To accomplish his purposes involves accomplishing them his way.

Saul and David were prime examples of this conundrum. Saul was told to wait for Samuel to come and offer sacrifices before going into battle, but Samuel arrived late. Saul took matters into his own hands and offered the sacrifices himself—against God's instructions. He saw the right goal but accomplished it in the wrong way. And God took away his kingdom.

As for David, he had two opportunities to open the door to his own kingship. He had already been chosen and anointed as

THE CITY GATE

City gates in the ancient world were more than entranceways and guard posts. They were the hub of the city. The gate was often the site of business transactions, legal hearings, councils of elders, and public speeches. It became a general term for the government and economy of a city—something Jesus had in mind when he declared that the gates of hell would not prevail against his church (Matt. 16:18). To capture the gates of a city was to possess the city itself.

That's why Boaz met the kinsman at the gate, explained the details of the situation in the presence of ten elders, acquired the rights to buy Naomi's family field and marry Ruth, and signified the transaction with a visible exchange of a sandal and an announcement in the presence of the people. When a deal was made in such a manner, it was as binding as a contract could get.

Saul's successor, so he knew it was God's will. And Saul, zealous about finding David to kill him, was clearly irrational and needed to be removed from Israel's throne. So when David had a perfect opportunity to kill Saul in a cave, he might well have thought that God had delivered his enemy into his hands. And when he sneaked into Saul's camp at night and found the king sleeping, he might have thought the same. But he knew God would not have him strike "the Lord's anointed," so he passed up his perfect opportunities and adhered to God's righteous standards. He refused short cuts. To fulfill God's purposes meant to do it God's way and in God's timing. And God eventually established David on the throne.

Boaz faced that choice too, and he passed the test. He wanted to marry Ruth, but he also wanted to adhere to God's law. Such details may have seemed unnecessary in the spiritual climate of Israel, but Boaz went by the book. And God honored his obedience by fulfilling his desire.

Laws Fulfilled: Ruth 4:1–12

Boaz was a masterful negotiator—at least on this issue so close to his heart. According to the law, Elimelech's old tract of land, his piece of the promise, must stay in his family. And not just any family member will do; the redeemer has to be the closest male relative of the deceased who is actually willing to buy it. With the field and the widow being legally inseparable in this redemption process, Boaz first puts forth the matter of the land. Someone has to do it, he indicates, so one of these men must fulfill his responsibility. Seeing an opportunity to expand his estate, the kinsman agrees.

Then Boaz moves on to the other small matter of the widow. He could have called her "that lovely, hard-working young

THE MAN WITH NO NAME

Every key character in the book of Ruth is identified by name except for one: the man who passed up an opportunity to become a member of the royal lineage of the Messiah. He didn't know the stakes were so high, of course, but the writer of Ruth makes a clear contrast between his self-interested protection of his family's inheritance and the selfless actions of Boaz. And what better way to prove that God honors those who go above and beyond their obligations according to the Law? The book ends with an impressive genealogy—a list of names—that serves as an exclamation point on the nameless man who missed his chance.

woman who has remained so faithful to Naomi," but he doesn't. No, she's simply "the dead man's widow" and, by the way, a Moabite, for those who hadn't heard. But she comes with the land—all or nothing.

The kinsman knows what that means. In order to keep the land as close to the deceased's line as possible, this widow must bear children—through him. The responsibility of natural fatherhood would be his, and the benefits of the inheritance would be theirs. And this transaction could eventually cause the redeemer's own inheritance to be split between his own children and these surrogate children of Elimelech. An extra wife and additional kids—that could get complicated. No, he decides. He'll pass.

The deal is accomplished. Boaz will own up to his levirate responsibilities and, if he must, marry this burdensome Moabite who comes inconveniently packaged with the land. Bethlehem's elders witness the transaction. It's a binding contract. And Boaz, who already owned plenty of land, walks away with what he really wanted: a beautiful new bride of noble character who will eventually bear his children.

Discuss

- What risk do you think Boaz took by paying such close attention to the legal process? How did God honor his concern for obeying the law?

  _____

  _____

  _____

- Think of a time when you've been tempted to take a short cut to God's will. What did you decide to do, and how did it turn out? Do you think God is more interested in our reaching his plans or in our obedience along the way? Why?

  _____

  _____

  _____

Hearts Fulfilled: Ruth 4:13–22

For the first time since chapter 1, the Lord is mentioned as an active agent in this story. It is he who has enabled Ruth to conceive. Of course, he enabled Ruth to wind up in Boaz's field, Boaz to notice her and treat her specially, and both of them to come together on the threshing floor for a momentous decision. But since his favor in 1:6 and Naomi's accusations in 1:21, he has either worked behind the scenes or invoked a potential blesser. Now he's the fulfiller of redemption and hope.

As for the women who once listened to Naomi's accusations, they now marvel at God's provision. Naomi had declared in 1:20 that she had left the Promised Land full and come back empty. But the larger story is that she left the Promised Land fleeing a famine and has been blessed with fullness and abundance upon her return. From an eternal perspective, she was empty from the beginning. Now she's a matriarch of the coming kings of Israel.

That's because Boaz and Ruth bear Obed, who fathers Jesse, who fathers David—making Naomi the great-great-grandmother of Israel's greatest king and a member of the lineage of Messiah. As far as the women of Bethlehem are concerned, God has provided Naomi a son. Her lineage is redeemed.

As for Ruth, God's message is clear: a foreign widow who acts faithfully is a more valuable member of the kingdom of God than seven Jewish sons who don't. Loving the God of Israel is a matter of the heart, not a matter of genetics or status or cultural baggage. Ruth, as unlikely as she was, is the kind of person on whom God's kingdom is built.

Discuss

• How might the story of Ruth have been used as an example during periods when Israel was in tension with other nations? How might it be used as an example for the church today?

_____

_____

_____

• Whose redemption was greater in this story: Ruth's or Naomi's? Whose do you most identify with? Why?

_____

_____

_____

A Case Study

Imagine: Before his untimely death last year, your quirky cousin worked for a nonprofit organization in an impoverished country. He had always been a little too offbeat for your taste—he even went "native" a few years back by practicing the customs of his adopted country and marrying a local. Now, out of the blue, his widow calls you. She traveled to your city in hopes of a better life, but she has nothing. No home, no money, no job, no skills. She can barely even speak English. You're the only one she knows—and, as far as you can tell, she's assuming you'll let her move in with you. After all, in her culture, that's what relatives do.

- Would you see this as a problem to deal with or as an opportunity to demonstrate the Lord's compassion?
- To what extent would you get involved in her life? What would you consider your obligations to be? How far out of your way would you go to accommodate her needs?
- What do you think the biblical response to this situation is?

An Everlasting Picture

Of all the *megillot*—the five scrolls read at feasts throughout the Jewish year—Joana's favorite is the scroll that will be read in the congregation today. The occasion is the Feast of Weeks, the harvest festival that falls fifty days after the Feast of First-fruits. Traditionally, it's also the holiday that commemorates that earthshaking day when God gave the Law to Israel on Mount Sinai, the day when the congregation of God's people made a commitment: "We will do everything the Lord has said to do" (Exod. 19:8). The sages saw it as Israel's betrothal to her God. The symbolism, Joana feels, is irresistible.

So Joana will listen closely today and savor the second *megillah*—the book of Ruth. It's no mystery that this is the scroll congregations have always read during the Feast of Weeks. It's a story of a commitment to God, an abundant harvest, and a betrothal. It represents everything Joana wants her marriage to be: holy, heaven-sent, and heartwarming.

The Feast of Weeks, or *Shavuot*, is also known as Pentecost. Jews from around the empire were gathered in Jerusalem one Pentecost long ago, and the Spirit of God fell on a group of believers gathered to worship and wait for the Messiah. The good news these believers proclaimed in various languages would mark the beginning of a vast and rapid expansion of God's people that would include Gentiles as well as Jews.

It's no coincidence that the Spirit came at a harvest festival; and it's fitting that the book Jews still read today at that festival is Ruth—a story of a Gentile who became one of God's people by betrothal to a man with an inheritance in the land. It's as if God was creating a picture over the centuries to represent his ultimate plan for the nations. He would bring a multiethnic harvest into his inheritance through a romantic redemption.

That's the big picture of God's purposes, and Ruth is a snapshot of it. Beyond the themes of commitment, faithfulness, hospitality, and God's provision, this story has implications

SHALOM

The Hebrew word for "peace" means much more than the absence of conflict. To wish *shalom* for someone is to wish a blessing of fullness, abundance, wholeness, contentment, rest, and joy. The story of Ruth is the story of *shalom* that was lost and then found again, a story of how God can bring *shalom* into the most chaotic, calamitous, and desperate of situations. By the end of the book, Naomi, Ruth, and Boaz have experienced the *shalom* of God—a picture of the "abundant life" Jesus would one day promise to those who follow him.

SHAVUOT

The book of Ruth's association with *Shavuot* (the Feast of Weeks, or Pentecost) comes from the season in which it takes place. It spans the barley harvest, which begins around the time of Passover, when the first fruits are offered, and lasts about seven weeks until *Shavuot*, when the end of the harvest is celebrated. In later writings, the Feast of Weeks was identified as the time when Israel received the Torah at Mount Sinai— essentially the same commitment Ruth made when she embraced Naomi's God. Interestingly, King David, Ruth's descendant, is traditionally said to have been born and to have died during the Feast of Weeks.

---

for missions and ministry too. It's a divine hint that God will often choose the least likely strangers to be his most fruitful friends.

The Gentile Light: Genesis 12:1–3; Isaiah 42:1–6

Even from the beginning, God's chosen people were to be a light to the nations. Throughout Scripture, God-fearing people everywhere were drawn to Israel's faith. There were Egyptians who left with Israel in the Exodus, a harlot of Jericho who joined God's people in the conquest of Canaan, Gentiles who served God during the ministries of Elijah and Elisha, a queen who came to Jerusalem to marvel at Solomon's wisdom and wealth, Assyrians who repented at Jonah's preaching, and Romans who aligned themselves with Jewish synagogues. The international, multiethnic, multilingual message of God's kingdom was not a New Testament innovation. God has always been relentless about drawing the world to himself.

Discuss

- Do you know anyone like Ruth—a pure heart in an un-expected place—whom God might be calling to play a significant part in his plan? If so, how can your hospitality help cultivate his or her calling?

_____

_____

_____

_____

_____

The Harvest: Deuteronomy 16:9–12; Acts 2:1–21

God calls and equips his people to be fruitful. Jesus made that clear through numerous parables and principles. His kingdom is in a long harvest season of gathering sheaves of grain from the fields. Like Ruth, we're invited into his fields to work. He makes sure we're protected from those who would harm us or send us away, and he leaves plenty of gleanings so we can gather with him.

Discuss

- Have you found the field(s) God has called you to labor in yet? If not, what steps can you take to allow him to guide you where he wants to?

_____

_____

_____

_____

_____

The Bride: Revelation 19:6–9

God's ultimate purpose for his people is like Boaz's ultimate purpose for Ruth: marriage and children. One gets the impression that God has been orchestrating the remarkable events of Ruth all along—across cultures, geographical boundaries, and adverse circumstances—in order to match Boaz and Ruth together. And one gets the impression from the Bible as a whole that he's been doing the same in bringing us to Jesus. Scripture is clear that God is preparing a bride for his Son; this is what all of history is leading up to. Like Ruth, the bride of Christ begins as a foreigner from an immoral land steeped in idolatry; but in our desolation, we commit to him and he takes us in. We go from forsaken widow to beloved bride, and the blessings of the kingdom are ours to enjoy.

Discuss

- The book of Ruth is a romance with a very happy ending. Do you think that's an accurate picture of life in this world? Why or why not? How well does it depict your hopes for an inheritance in God's kingdom?

_____

_____

_____

_____

_____

_____

A Case Study

Imagine: A mysterious stranger—an angel perhaps?—appears to you and makes an amazing offer: God would like to give you a lasting legacy and an eternal testimony in the annals of his work on earth. There's a cost involved; God is going to rearrange your life. The stranger won't tell you all the details up front, but it's clear that you'll have to leave home and live in a foreign culture. It won't be easy. You'll be taken out of some old relationships and placed in new ones. You may lose everything you've staked your security and hopes on. But the promise is that you'll have all that and more. Your story will be told for generations. You'll go down in eternal history as a key player in God's ultimate plan.

- Do you think the cost of this offer is worth the benefit you'll receive? Why or why not?
- How does this offer reflect Ruth's situation? How does it reflect the decision anyone makes when they come to Christ?
- In what ways is this a daily decision believers must make?

Conclusion

The story of Ruth is a comfort to anyone going through a hard time. Our nature in a crisis is to hover between Naomi's two identities: will our name end up being "pleasant" or "bitter"? Will God redeem the worst of times? And what will redemption look like—a consolation prize or an even more blessed life than before?

For Naomi, Ruth, and Boaz, the fullness of life after God restores it was better than the fullness of their lives before things went sour. The death of Naomi's and Ruth's husbands eventually led to a greater blessing than they would have experienced in Moab. It's a story of faithful people who stuck with God and his people. In the end, Boaz and Ruth enjoyed a fulfilling, fruitful marriage, and Naomi had her inheritance restored to her in greater measure. It's a picture of how God works; he can turn any loss into a greater gain.

Ultimately, the book of Ruth is about any human being who leaves everything behind to believe in Israel's God and the Redeemer he has provided. Ours is the genuine rags-to-riches story for which all others serve as hints and shadows. As sinners in a fallen world, we lost it all, but as committed followers of God, we get it all back and more.

Our story is Naomi's story: from bitterness and despair to joy and fullness; our story is Boaz's story: from waiting in the wings to a lasting legacy; our story is Ruth's story: from loss to commitment to betrothal to the ultimate Bridegroom.

And for all of us who believe, the story ends with fruit-fulness. Actually, it doesn't exactly "end" at all. God's *shalom* is never-ending—a legacy that extends forever in his eternal Promised Land.

Leader's Notes

Session 1

Deuteronomy 25:5–10. "God's desire was for his blessings to extend to a thousand generations—i.e., forever." This desire is found in Exodus 20:5–6 and Deuteronomy 5:9–10 and 7:9. (It's also referred to in 1 Chronicles 16:5 and Psalm 105:8.) The term "a thousand" in the Bible generally means "more than you can count," as in Psalm 50:10: "Every animal in the forest is mine, and the cattle on a thousand hills."

Session 2

Ruth 1:19–22, second discussion question. This is designed to make the point that we most need God's deliverance in a crisis, which also happens to be the time we're most likely to question God's power or love. Help guide participants to the realization that these situations are platforms for God to show his power and love most vividly.

The Moabite Stigma. The background of each incident in this sidebar is fascinating. You can read about Lot and his daughters in Genesis 19:29–38; about Balak, Balaam, and Moabite women in Numbers 22–25; and about oppressive King Eglon and his demise in Judges 3.

Session 3

Ruth 2:1-13, second discussion question. This question deals with the downtrodden at a community level—i.e., how a particular church should respond to those in need. If there's time, and if it can be done without digressing too far from Ruth's primary themes, consider expanding this discussion by posing the question of how Christians should inform national policy regarding immigration today. What would a biblical response to current immigration issues look like?

Session 5

The story of Saul's impatient sacrifice mentioned in the introduction to this session is found in 1 Samuel 13. The two examples of David's patience are found in 1 Samuel 24 and 26.

Session 6

A Case Study. This example intentionally leaves a lot of "unknowns" in the story because that's how God calls us forward—with great costs, greater promises, and lots of uncertainty about the specifics. Your group may naturally gravitate toward well-known situations in their minds as they read this scenario: a missionary calling, a conversion in a gospel-unfriendly land, a drastically new career path, etc. Those are helpful points of reference, but also help participants see that this kind of proposal from God applies in some degree to every one of us when we come to him in faith.

Bibliography

Alexander, David, and Pat Alexander. *Zondervan Handbook to the Bible*. Grand Rapids: Zondervan, 1999.

Berlin, Adele, Marc Zvi Brettler, and Michael Fishbane, eds. *The Jewish Study Bible*. Oxford and New York: Oxford University Press, 2004.

Chilton, Bruce, et al. *The Cambridge Companion to the Bible*. Cambridge and New York: Cambridge University Press, 1997.

Dumbrell, William J. *The Faith of Israel: A Theological Survey of the Old Testament*. Grand Rapids: Baker Academic, 2002.

Hoerth, Alfred J. *Archaeology and the Old Testament*. Grand Rapids: Baker Books, 1998.

Kaiser, Walter C., Jr., and Duane Garrett, eds. *Archaeological Study Bible*. Grand Rapids: Zondervan, 2006.

Matthews, Victor H., and Don C. Benjamin. *The Social World of Ancient Israel*. Peabody, MA: Hendrickson, 1993.

Shanks, Herschel, ed. *Ancient Israel: From Abraham to the Roman Destruction of the Temple*. Upper Saddle River, NJ: Prentice Hall, 1999.

Snell, Daniel C. *Life in the Ancient Near East*. New Haven: Yale University Press, 1997.

Telushkin, Joseph. *Biblical Literacy: The Most Important People, Events, and Ideas of the Hebrew Bible.* New York: William Morrow, 1997.

Walton, John H., Victor H. Matthews, and Mark W. Chavalas. *The IVP Bible Background Commentary: Old Testament.* Downers Grove, IL: InterVarsity Press, 2000.

WALK THRU THE BIBLE®

Helping people everywhere
live God's Word

For more than three decades, Walk Thru the Bible has created discipleship materials and cultivated leadership networks that together are reaching millions of people through live seminars, print publications, audiovisual curricula, and the Internet. Known for innovative methods and high-quality resources, we serve the whole body of Christ across denominational, cultural, and national lines. Through our strong and cooperative international partnerships, we are strategically positioned to address the church's greatest need: developing mature, committed, and spiritually reproducing believers.

Walk Thru the Bible communicates the truths of God's Word in a way that makes the Bible readily accessible to anyone. We are committed to developing user-friendly resources that are Bible centered, of excellent quality, life changing for individuals, and catalytic for churches, ministries, and movements; and we are committed to maintaining our global reach through strategic partnerships while adhering to the highest levels of integrity in all we do.

Walk Thru the Bible partners with the local church worldwide to fulfill its mission, helping people "walk thru" the Bible with greater clarity and understanding. Live seminars and small group curricula are taught in over 45 languages by more than 80,000 people in more than 70 countries, and more than 100 million devotionals have been packaged into daily magazines, books, and other publications that reach over five million people each year.

Walk Thru the Bible
4201 North Peachtree Road
Atlanta, GA 30341-1207
770-458-9300
www.walkthru.org

Read the entire Bible in one year, thanks to the systematic reading plan in the best-selling **Daily Walk** devotional.

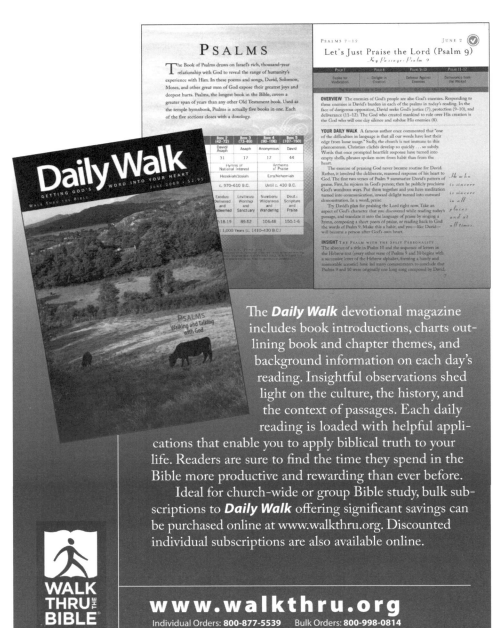

The **Daily Walk** devotional magazine includes book introductions, charts outlining book and chapter themes, and background information on each day's reading. Insightful observations shed light on the culture, the history, and the context of passages. Each daily reading is loaded with helpful applications that enable you to apply biblical truth to your life. Readers are sure to find the time they spend in the Bible more productive and rewarding than ever before.

Ideal for church-wide or group Bible study, bulk subscriptions to **Daily Walk** offering significant savings can be purchased online at www.walkthru.org. Discounted individual subscriptions are also available online.

WALK THRU THE BIBLE

www.walkthru.org